Genre | Historical Fiction

M000249653

Essential Question
Why is it important to keep a record of the past?

Nonna's Recipes

by Paul Mason
illustrated by Jan Lieffering

Chapter 1
A Whole World Away 2

Chapter 2
Grandmother's Recipes .6

Chapter 3
The Shop 10

Chapter 4
Success 13

Respond to Reading 16

PAIRED READ Little Italy 17

Focus on Literary Elements 20

A Whole World Away

Francesca stared out the window as a delivery cart pulled up at the small hotel across the street. On the back of the carriage, Francesca read, "T-H-E   P-E-N-N-S-Y-L-V-A-N-I-A I-N-N."

"Inn what?" Francesca thought. It didn't make sense, but then again, she felt that her English was hopeless. She'd only been in the country a month.

"Still gazing out the window?" Francesca's mother teased.

"It all looks so different!" Francesca exclaimed. Compared with their small village in Italy, this town seemed huge.

"Are you happy we came?" her mother asked.

Francesca nodded. She was glad their family had a chance to start a new life. After all, they had worked so hard and endured a difficult journey to get to America.

Despite that, Francesca still woke up every morning thinking about her grandmother, Nonna, who was a whole world away.

Francesca's mom realized that her daughter was feeling lonely. "Let's go to the park. We might see Adriana there."

"Sure!" Francesca grinned. Adriana was her first friend in the neighborhood.

The two of them went downstairs, past the empty shop below their apartment. They showed obedience for the traffic rules by watching out for carriages before they crossed the busy street. They had already learned that crossing the road in this town could be treacherous.

Francesca and her mother found Adriana and some of the other children and their mothers at the park. It was in the heart of the Italian neighborhood—a refuge of green in the busy city. Francesca ran off to play with her new friends while her mom talked to the other mothers.

"Catch me if you can!" Francesca called to Adriana.

The girls ran until they were out of breath, then collapsed on a park bench.

"What do you miss most about Italy?" Adriana asked, panting.

"My nonna," replied Francesca.

Adriana nodded. "Yes, I miss my grandparents, too, but what I would do for some *grissini*!"

Francesca laughed. "You miss breadsticks?"

Adriana giggled. "They're my absolute favorite. You can't get any here."

"No problem," Francesca said with a shrug. "I used to make them all the time with Nonna. I'll make you some later."

That night, Francesca's
father came home
exhausted after spending
another day looking for
work. He'd been all over
town—to the building
sites, the steel mill, and
the lumberyard. At each
place, he'd been completely
ignored.

"I just don't understand
it," Francesca's dad said as
he took off his hat with a
sigh. "We were told there
was a lot of work here,
but I can't find a job."
He shook his head. "I'm
a stonemason. I should be
able to get building work.
I'm running out of ideas."

Francesca's mom wiped her hands
and left Francesca to finish the baking. "I'm sure
something will come up," her mom said with a smile.
She certainly hoped something would. She detested
seeing her husband so worried and so tired.

Chapter 2

Grandmother's Recipes

It turned out that Francesca's mom was right—but not in the way they expected. The idea came to Francesca when she was at the park. She'd made grissini for Adriana as she'd promised. As soon as Adriana opened the paper bag and started sharing them with her mother, they were surrounded by the other children.

"Grissini!" the children exclaimed. "May we have one, please?"

With a nod of her head, Adriana broke up the breadsticks and handed out the pieces. "Is there any chance you could make more grissini?" she pleaded with Francesca.

"Why not?" said Francesca, laughing. Then it struck her. Why couldn't they make a whole lot more?

After dinner that night, Francesca told her father about taking the breadsticks to the park and her idea.

"A bakery?" Her father was surprised. "There must be plenty of bakeries in this town."

"Bakeries, yes," said Francesca, "but no Italian ones. Mama and I had a look, and we couldn't find a single one."

Her mother nodded. "She's right."

"But what do we know about bakeries?" her dad asked. "I work with stone, not bread," he said with a little chuckle.

"We have this," said Francesca, taking a book off the kitchen counter. It was Nonna's recipe book—her gift to the family, so that even in America, they could still taste her cooking and remember home.

Francesca turned the pages of the precious book. In Nonna's messy handwriting there were recipes for breads such as *focaccia* and *ciabatta*, as well as pastries and pasta.

The kitchen was the heart of Nonna's home, and each page of her recipe book brought a piece of it to life in their tiny apartment in America.

Francesca smiled as she remembered lunches at Nonna's house. The family gathered around the table, and the small cottage was filled with the smell of fresh bread. On holidays, the children were allowed to have a sweet *cannoli*, or pastry, from the small tower of cannoli that Nonna had made.

Francesca could picture Nonna right now. Her sleeves would be rolled up, and she'd probably be in the kitchen making bread, her hands white with flour.

Francesca's father sighed happily as he found a favorite recipe. "You know, there is so much of our home in this book. Each dish depicts a different time, a different place." He closed the book. The spark was back in his eyes. "Francesca, I think a bakery may be the answer."

Chapter 3
The Shop

Over the next week, Francesca's father put his plan into action. The family had managed to scrape together enough money to get by, but the longer it took to set up the bakery, the more of their savings they would use.

Francesca's father approached the landlord about the empty shop under their apartment. It used to be a small café.

Fortune seemed to be smiling on the family. Not only was the shop still available, but because they lived in the building and they came from the same region of Italy as the landlord, he gave them a good deal.

Francesca and her mother cleaned out the dusty cafe, wiping down the counters, clearing out the small cupboards, and discarding old papers. Francesca's dad bought the equipment and the ingredients they needed to make bread and pastries.

"Make sure you get the best olive oil we can afford," Francesca's mom told him. "Nonna always used good oil."

"And the flour has to be fine and strong," said Francesca. "Nonna always had good flour."

"And make sure the eggs are fresh," added her mother. "Nonna—"

"Always used fresh eggs," her father said with a laugh. "I know, I know."

At the end of a hard week's work, the shop was ready for business. The family watched as the sign writer painted the name on the window in neat gold writing: "Ricette della Nonna, Panetteria."

"Grandma's Recipes Bakery. A good name for a bakery, and it sounds nice," said the sign writer.

"You must come and get some ciabatta tomorrow," said Francesca's dad.

"Fresh ciabatta … I can't wait!" the man said, laughing.

Now that the bakery was ready for business, there was a problem. How would people know that there was an Italian bakery in town? There was absolutely no money left for any advertising.

Again it was Francesca who had an idea. "Let's make some grissini, and then Mama and I can hand it out door-to-door for free and tell everyone about the bakery."

"And we can always take it to the families in the park," added her mom.

Francesca's dad squeezed his wife's hand and smiled at his daughter. "Let's get to work."

Chapter 4
Success

On the day the bakery opened, it was still dark when Francesca's parents got out of bed. They fired up the oven and began making dough. Though it was early, they were wide-awake and nervous about what the day would bring.

By the warm glow of the lamp, her parents got to work. They sifted flour, kneaded dough, and quickly found their way around the shop. As dawn broke, they were joined by Francesca and were grateful for the extra pair of hands.

"I'll put the bread out on display," offered Francesca. With each loaf of ciabatta and focaccia that she stacked, Francesca felt her Nonna was close to her. "She'd be proud," thought Francesca, "that her recipes have filled this shop and given us a chance at a new life. I'll write and tell her."

As the street began to show signs of life, Francesca's father threw open the bakery doors. He waited nervously on the sidewalk to see if there would be any customers.

"I hope we've made the right decision," said Francesca's mother.

Her husband squeezed her hand. "I know we have. As soon as the smell of fresh bread hits the air, we'll have some customers."

Sure enough, a man soon stopped outside their shop. "Ah, so this is the new Italian bakery. My eldest son, Roberto, brought home some grissini yesterday."

"Yes, that was a small gift from us," said Francesca's mother.

"Do you have biscotti?" the man asked hopefully.

"Come this way," said Francesca's dad, smiling.

Their first customer was soon joined by another, and then another, all asking for Francesca. The sign writer came back with his wife. The landlord came to wish them good luck. Soon the shop was full of chattering and talk about Italy, with everyone sharing memories about the places they'd left behind.

Adriana and her mother stopped by to say hello.

"You can have a bag of grissini for free," said Francesca's mom, "because you helped Francesca come up with the idea for the bakery in the first place."

By the end of the day, the shelves were almost bare, and the family was exhausted. Francesca's dad whistled happily as he and her mom cleaned the counters and got the baking trays ready for the following morning. Francesca sat perched on a stool, giving her legs a rest. But there was still time for one last customer.

"Ricette della Nonna. What a lovely name," said the woman as she breathed in the air of the shop. "I must bring you some of my nonna's recipes. She made the most wonderful *piadina romagnola*—you know the flat bread?"

"Yes, we'd like to have that recipe," replied Francesca's mother.

The woman smiled. "Where would we be without our grandmothers' recipes?"

Francesca's dad gave Francesca a big smile. "Where indeed?"

Respond to Reading

Summarize

Use important details from *Nonna's Recipes* to summarize the story. Your graphic organizer may help you.

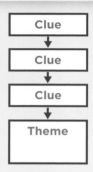

Text Evidence

1. How can you tell that this story is historical fiction? **GENRE**

2. How does Nonna's recipe book help the family settle into their new home? **THEME**

3. Use context clues to define the word *piece* on page 8. What is a homophone for *piece*? What does the homophone mean? **HOMOPHONES**

4. Write about how the family and the other characters feel connected to their past through the bakery. Explain how the details about this connection help you identify the story's theme. **WRITE ABOUT READING**

Compare Texts
Read about Italian immigration to the United States.

Little Italy

In the late 1800s, hundreds of thousands of Italian people immigrated to the United States. Many had struggled to earn a living in Italy.

At first, most immigrants were young men who worked as laborers. They would save some money and then return home to Italy. These workers were nicknamed "birds of passage" because they made these trips between the United States and Italy many times.

Archive Pics/Alamy

17

Over time, women and families also immigrated to the United States. Italian immigrants usually lived alongside other Italian people. Their neighborhoods often became known as Little Italy.

When families arrived, some opened stores and shops. For example, Saverio Spadafora and his wife, Maria Pullano, settled in Reading, Pennsylvania. They lived in an Italian neighborhood with their children, and in 1903, they opened the first Italian bakery in the city.

Bain News Service/George Grantham Bain Collection (Library of Congress)

Little Italies

Italian culture thrived within the Little Italies. The immigrants brought to the United States the things they missed from home, such as theater and other kinds of entertainment. Newspapers and Italian bookstores opened, and people met at coffeehouses to talk and tell stories about home.

Some Italian people sold goods from street stalls.

Italian Settlement in the United States as of 1890

Mountain High Maps/Digital Wisdom

Key
● Areas where Italian immigrants settled

A large number of Italian immigrants settled in cities such as New York, Chicago, Philadelphia, and Boston. Over time, many people ran their own businesses or stores. The Italian immigrants and their descendants have made important contributions to the United States in areas such as food, sports, business, and the arts.

Make Connections

Why did Italian immigrants choose to live close to each other? ESSENTIAL QUESTION

Use the map above to find some areas, other than Pennsylvania, where Francesca's family might have started an Italian bakery. TEXT TO TEXT

19

Focus on
Literary Elements

Mood Writers use words to help create a mood or atmosphere in a story. This helps readers to visualize and understand the characters' actions and feelings. Writers can use words to create a mood that is cheerful, sad, anxious, scary, or dreamy.

Read and Find Reread page 4. Francesca and Adriana are happy, and they giggle and laugh. The writer has used words to create a happy mood. Reread page 5. Francesca's dad is described as *worried* and *tired*. These words create a gloomy mood.

Your Turn

Think of four different moods a writer might want to use in a story. For each mood, make a word map. Write the name of a mood in the middle of a circle. Draw lines out from the circle and add words that you connect with that mood. For example, if the mood word is *happy*, you could add words such as *giggle*, *laugh*, *grin*, *tickle*, or *glad*. Share your word maps and save them to help you create atmosphere in your writing.